The Story of

Billy McNeill

JAMES MCIVOR *and* MICHAEL MARTIN

passing on the passion

Benchmark Books Ltd
50 Shuna Place
Newton Mearns
Glasgow G77 6TN

E: enquiries@benchmarkbooks.co.uk
W: www.benchmarkbooks.co.uk

1st edition 2008

ISBN 978-0-9554950-4-5

Illustrations by Doreen Shaw

Thanks to Billy McNeill, Bertie Auld and all at Celtic Football Club

Printed by Oriental Press, Dubai

Foreword

It was a real honour to be asked to write the foreword to *The Story of Billy McNeill*.

I first met Billy in 1958 when he was all knees and elbows and I didn't even know what position he played.

The next reserve game there he was in the dressing room, ready to play at centre-back. As usual I was looking up to him – and that was when he was sitting down and I was standing!

Billy had a real confidence in his own ability without being arrogant and was Celtic through and through – it was a privilege to play with him and I knew even then that he could go on to become a Celtic great.

When I left Celtic Park in 1961, Billy was just a Bhoy. When I returned in 1965 he was a man, he was big Cesar.

Billy could have left Celtic for any club in England but he stayed and became an ever-present – he was a strong character, physically and mentally, and he had a huge presence.

The turning point for Celtic was winning the 1965 Scottish Cup final – and of course I scored twice that day and big Billy got the winner.

Two years he later he was lifting the European Cup.

Big Jock needed someone like himself on the pitch, he needed a leader. That someone was Billy.

Young supporters today are beginning to discover what it is that makes Celtic the greatest football club in the world and by reading this wonderful book they will discover that Billy McNeill represents everything that is great about Celtic.

He was a great team-mate, a great captain and a great manager but most of all he is a great pal.

Bertie Auld

BILLY McNEILL is the greatest Celtic captain of all time.

In an incredible playing career he won nine Scottish league titles, seven Scottish Cups and six League Cups.

And in 1967 he became the first British player to lift the greatest trophy of them all – the European Cup.

Billy also managed Celtic twice, leading his Bhoys to four league championships, three Scottish Cups and one League Cup.

William McNeill was born on 2 March 1940. His grandparents were from Lithuania and had hoped to emigrate to America but ended up in Scotland by mistake.

Had they got their wish to move to the United States, Billy might have ended up playing baseball or basketball.

But fate decided that he would be a legend for Glasgow Celtic – not the **Boston** Celtics!

Billy grew up in the Lanarkshire town of Bellshill with his mum, Ellen, and dad, Jimmy. Until Billy was six they lived with Billy's Lithuanian grandparents and his mum's sister, Grace.

The house was cramped, and had no inside toilet, but Billy was very happy.

Jimmy McNeill was a soldier and taught Billy about hard work and discipline. Like most army men, Jimmy always walked with a straight back and a puffed-out chest. It was an example that Billy would follow all his life, on and off the football pitch.

Because Jimmy was often away from home with the army, it was Billy's Aunt Grace who took him to his first football match.

It was in October 1949, and Billy was nine years old.

Billy and Grace stood on the terraces of the Jungle (now the North Stand) to see Celtic beat Aberdeen 4–2.

It was an unforgettable day for Billy – especially as Grace lost her shoe in the Jungle and had to go home on the bus with only one shoe!

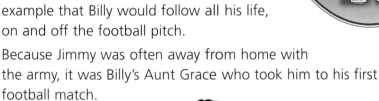

PLAYING HONOURS

Nine Scottish League Championships
1965–66, 1966–67, 1967–68, 1968–69, 1969–70, 1970–71, 1971–72, 1972–73, 1973–74

Seven Scottish Cups
1964–65, 1966–67, 1968–69, 1970–71, 1971–72, 1973–74, 1974–75

Six Scottish League Cups
1965–66, 1966–67, 1967–68, 1968–69, 1969–70, 1974–75

One European Cup
1966–67

MANAGERIAL HONOURS

Four Scottish League Championships
1978–79, 1980–81, 1981–82, 1987–88

Three Scottish Cups
1979–80, 1987–88, 1988–89

One Scottish League Cup
1982–83

Billy used to play football on the streets with his pals for hours on end, night after night, and progressed to playing for local teams.

He soon began making a name for himself on the football pitch and when he was 17 his school, Our Lady's High in Motherwell, reached the Scottish Schools Cup final.

It was his first national cup final – but it would not be his last.

Unfortunately, Billy scored an own goal in the game, which ended in a 1–1 draw, but he would enjoy many great days at Hampden Park.

There was supposed to be a replay but it never took place because the teams could not agree on where to play the match!

The top clubs in Britain had been impressed by the towering defender and Billy had the chance to sign for Arsenal, Manchester United, Newcastle, Clyde and Partick Thistle in 1957.

Then one night in May of that year there was a knock at the door of Billy's parents' home.

Standing there were Eddie McCardle, a Celtic scout, and another man called Jock Stein.

Jock had been a great Celtic captain and was now in charge of the reserve team.

He had seen Billy play for Scotland schoolboys and had come to ask him to join Celtic.

It did not take long for Billy to sign on – even though Jock, a tough character, warned him that he would get a 'skelp' if he stepped out of line!

Big Jock was a very clever man but not even he could have known then that, together, they would go on to become the most successful Celtic manager and captain of all time.

Before Billy made it at Celtic Park he was loaned out to a team called Blantyre Victoria for a season.

Blantyre Vics play in Scotland's 'junior' leagues. They may be called juniors but the players in these leagues are not any younger than normal. In fact, you have to be strong and hard to survive in the juniors – so Billy was sent there to toughen himself up for first-team football. A year later he was back and on 23 August 1958 he made his debut in a 2–0 League Cup win over Clyde.

Despite only being 18, Billy did not look out of place alongside Celtic greats like Charlie Tully, Bertie Peacock, Bobby Evans, Bobby Collins and Willie Fernie.

Jock Stein had been forced to stop playing because of an ankle injury two years earlier – which is why he was now in charge of the reserve side.

Jock was also from Lanarkshire and he would take a special interest in fellow 'Shire Bhoys like Billy and a young lad named John Clark.

In those days even the great Jock Stein travelled home by bus after training.

He made Billy and John wait with him at the stop until his bus arrived. As they waited Jock would tell them fascinating stories about football and give them wise words of advice. The valuable lessons would never be forgotten.

By 1960, Billy was the first-choice centre-half at Celtic – but that same year Big Jock was allowed to leave the club to become manager of Dunfermline.

The following year Celtic made it to the Scottish Cup final … and lost to Jock's Dunfermline.

It was still a season to remember for Billy as he won his first cap for Scotland, against England, and also met his future wife. Liz Callaghan was a dancer on a popular television programme called *The White Heather Club* – a 1960s version of *Strictly Come Dancing*.

Liz and Billy got engaged the next year, and married in June 1963. That same year Billy was given the chance to join the great Tottenham Hotspur side that was dominating English football.

Spurs had just become the first British side to win a European trophy, thumping Atletico Madrid 5–1 in the European Cup Winners' Cup final.

But not even the chance to star alongside legendary players like Danny Banchflower, Dave Mackay and Jimmy Greaves could pull Billy away from his beloved Celtic.

He had yet to win a trophy at Celtic but it would not take long for Billy to realise he had made the right decision …

CESAR THE NICKNAME

Many fans think that Billy is named Cesar after Julius Caesar because, like the Roman emperor, he was such a great leader.

But Billy was jokingly named after Hollywood actor Cesar Romano during a trip to the cinema with his Celtic team-mates in 1961.

The Celtic players were all big Frank Sinatra fans and went to see his famous movie Ocean's Eleven, *which featured Cesar Romano as the getaway car driver.*

Billy was the oldest of the group of friends and, because he was the only one to have a car, team-mate John Colrane jokingly called him 'Big Cesar' and it stuck.

People still call Billy 'Cesar' to this day.

In March 1965, Jock Stein returned to Celtic and changed the club forever.

Within a month he led his Bhoys to the Scottish Cup final against his old side Dunfermline.

The Pars twice went ahead but Celtic fought back bravely with two goals from midfield dynamo Bertie Auld.

In the final minute, and with the sides level at 2–2, Charlie Gallagher swung over a corner and Billy rose majestically to send an unstoppable header into the back of the net. The Scottish Cup was coming home to Paradise for the first time in 11 years.

It was the first of many great days under the best manager Scottish football has ever seen …

Just five months later Celtic beat Rangers 2–0 to lift the League Cup.

And when they hammered their oldest rivals 5–1 in January 1966 there was a feeling that Celtic could clinch the league title for the first time in 12 long years.

They did, but they had to wait until the very last minute of the last game to make sure. A Bobby Lennox goal in the 90th minute gave the Hoops a 1–0 win over Motherwell to leave them two points ahead of Rangers.

Little did they know that the league flag would continue to fly at Celtic Park for another nine years.

NINE IN A ROW

Billy captained Celtic as they became the first club in the world to win nine league championships in a row.

The Bhoys had not won the league for 12 years before finally winning it at Motherwell's Fir Park in 1966.

Just 12 months later, in 1967, Celtic won every competition they entered and clinched the league title by drawing 2–2 with Rangers at Ibrox with Jimmy Johnstone scoring both goals.

Incredibly, each title win during nine a row was clinched away from home. Celtic fans still sing about winning nine in a row – and dream of one day winning ten!

They also made their mark in Europe that year and Big Jock came up against an old Lanarkshire pal as Celtic drew Bill Shankly's Liverpool in the semi-final of the European Cup Winners' Cup.

Celtic won the first leg 1–0 and Bobby Lennox had a perfectly good goal wrongly disallowed at Anfield before the Reds ran out 2–1 winners on aggregate.

Important lessons had been learned, though, and season 1966–67 was to be the greatest in Billy's career and in Celtic's history …

Big Jock began the campaign by rewarding his stars with a luxury five-week tour of Canada and the USA. The players soon became best pals on and off the pitch.

The bond was so strong that it made Jock's Bhoys unstoppable that season.

BILLY AND SCOTLAND

Billy played for his country 29 times and had many great days in the dark blue of Scotland.

But his first game for the national team was one he would never forget – for all the wrong reasons – as Scotland were humiliated 9–3 by England at Wembley.

*What was supposed to be a proud day for Billy and his family turned into a disaster as everything that could go wrong **did** go wrong.*

But 12 months later Billy and Scotland got their revenge by beating the Auld Enemy 2–0 at Hampden. It was the first home win against England in 25 long years.

Billy loved playing for his country and scored three goals – against Poland, Wales and Cyprus.

His last game was a 1-0 defeat to England in the home international championship of 1972.

The Hoops won the League Cup, the Glasgow Cup, the Scottish Cup and held on to the league championship.

But they were not satisfied with being the best in Scotland – they wanted to be the kings of Europe too.

Celtic had already knocked out French side Nantes and Swiss champions FC Zurich when Vojvodina came to Glasgow for the quarter-final of the European Cup.

The Yugoslavs were one goal up from the first leg and when Stevie Chalmers scored for Celtic it looked like the tie would go to a replay.

But in the very last minute Jimmy Johnstone forced a corner and when the ball was swung over Billy rose above everyone to head home one of the most dramatic goals ever seen at Celtic Park.

Celtic then saw off Czechoslovakian champions Dukla Prague to reach the final of the European Cup.

And so it was on to Lisbon for the biggest game in the club's history … and a game that would change Billy's life forever.

No one expected Celtic to beat the champions of Italy, Inter Milan – and when the Bhoys lost a goal after seven minutes it looked like the dream was dying.

But Big Jock's Bhoys never gave up and, roared on by 25,000 travelling fans, they attacked, attacked and attacked.

Tommy Gemmell scored a wonder goal to equalise just after the hour mark and with five minutes to go Stevie Chalmers netted the winner.

Celtic were the champions of Europe and Billy became the first British player to lift the famous trophy.

To this day, Billy and his fellow Lisbon Lions have a special place in the hearts of all Celtic fans.

LISBON LIONS

The Lisbon Lions are the greatest Celtic team of all time but they could not have won the European Cup without their inspirational captain, Billy McNeill.

After Celtic beat Inter Milan in Lisbon, Portugal, on 25 May 1967, Billy became the first British player to lift club football's greatest prize.

Before 1967 only teams from Spain, Portugal or Italy had won the European Cup.

Billy played a captain's role throughout the competition and he scored the winning goal against Vojvodina in the quarter-final with a bullet header in the very last minute.

The Lisbon Lions are: Ronnie Simpson, Jim Craig, Tommy Gemmell, Bobby Murdoch, Billy McNeill, John Clark, Jimmy Johnstone, Willie Wallace, Stevie Chalmers, Bertie Auld and Bobby Lennox.

Celtic continued to dominate Scottish football and won the league again in 1968 and 1969.

They also reached the final of the Scottish Cup in 1969 where they met city rivals Rangers.

The Gers defenders had been warned to watch Billy at corners but with just two minutes on the clock he headed home the opening goal … from a corner!

His marker – a young lad name Alex Ferguson – could only look on in horror and Billy would go on to lift the Cup after an easy 4–0 victory.

The following season Celtic were on the march in Europe again and were drawn against Benfica in the quarter-final of the European Cup.

They won 3–0 at home – then lost 3–0 in Lisbon. In those days there was no extra time or penalties so, incredibly, the game was to be decided by the toss of a coin.

Billy's stomach was churning as he walked into the referee's room along with the Benfica captain.

He knew that if he made the wrong call he would have to go back and tell his team-mates they were out of Europe.

As the referee flicked the coin into the air Billy realised he had to say something, so he shouted 'heads'.

He breathed a huge sigh of relief when he looked down and saw the 'heads' side of the coin facing him as it came to rest on the floor.

Celtic were through to the semi-final – where they would meet English champions Leeds United.

They won the first leg at Elland Road thanks to a George Connolly goal after just 45 seconds.

Then, despite having an ankle injury, Billy skippered the side for the return leg at Hampden Park in front of a record crowd of 136,505.

Billy Bremner stunned the home support by putting Leeds in front and levelling the tie.

But the Scottish champions were too strong for the best in England and goals from John Hughes and Bobby Murdoch saw Celtic through to their second European Cup final in three years.

Sadly, Celtic lost that game 2–1 to Feyenoord from the Netherlands.

Manchester United wanted to sign
Billy in 1972 but Big Jock persuaded
him to stay. Led by their inspirational
captain, Celtic continued to be
kings of Scotland winning nine
titles in a row – a world
record at the time.

Billy was honoured with
an MBE from the
Queen and then on
3 May 1975, after 13
years as captain, he
pulled on the famous
hooped jersey for
the last time in a
competitive match.

Thankfully, Celtic
beat Airdrie 3–1
in the Scottish
Cup final to give
Billy the perfect
send-off.

But Cesar was not finished with football and after a brief spell as a businessman he became manager of Clyde.

His great work there was soon spotted by Aberdeen and Billy was offered the manager's job at Pittodrie.

Billy gave a boy named Alex McLeish his first team debut, playing him alongside another youngster, Willie Miller.

And he also signed Gordon Strachan from Dundee.

The Dons were runners-up to Rangers in the league and the Scottish Cup in Billy's first season.

Then he was offered the chance to return to his beloved Celtic as manager …

Rangers had won the treble the year before and Billy's job was to get the Hoops back to the top.

And in his first season back he did just that after one of the most dramatic title deciders of all time.

Rangers arrived at Celtic Park on 5 May 1979 needing just a draw to clinch the title again.

They went 1–0 ahead and things got worse when Johnny Doyle was sent off.

But Billy's Celtic sides never knew they were beaten and they battled back to win the match 4–2.

As the ecstatic Hoops fans sang afterwards, 'Ten men won the league!'

In five years as boss, Billy led Celtic to three league championships, one Scottish Cup and a League Cup.

But by 1983 he decided it was time to move on and he took over at Manchester City.

He took City from the old English Division Two (now called the Championship) into Division One (now called the Premier League) and helped them stay there.

Billy briefly took over at Aston Villa but by the start of season 1987–88 Celtic had again lost their grip on the title to big-spending Rangers and they needed a new manager.

Once again, they called on the club's greatest ever captain to save the day ...

Celtic were 100 years old but few people expected them to win a trophy in their centenary season.

Rangers had spent millions signing the top stars from England – including the English captain, Terry Butcher.

But Billy always believes Celtic will win and when he signed Andy Walker from Motherwell and Frank McAvennie from West Ham he knew he had two strikers who would score plenty of goals.

Great players like Tommy Burns, Roy Aitken, Paul McStay, Peter Grant and Pat Bonner ensured that Celtic not only won the league – they also lifted the Scottish Cup.

Billy said at the time: 'There is a fairytale about this club.'

And in 1988, against all the odds, he made that fairytale come true for the Celtic fans – it was the best birthday present ever, the double in their beloved club's centenary season.

Billy won the Scottish Cup the following year – again beating Rangers – but he left Paradise in 1991.

Billy remains involved in football to this day and regularly appears on TV and radio as well as writing a weekly column for a newspaper.

In 2001 he became one of the first members of the Scottish Sports Hall of Fame. This showed that Scottish people saw Billy as one of their greatest sportsmen of all time.

Billy is a famous and well-loved character in European football, too. In 2007 UEFA – the people in charge of football in Europe – asked him to present medals to Sevilla when they won the UEFA Cup at Hampden Park.

Billy is still adored by Celtic fans everywhere, and supporters clubs all over the world regularly invite him to go and visit them as their guest of honour. Billy loves to meet the fans and tries to go to as many of the supporters' parties as he possibly can.

Having made more than 800 appearances for the club, leading them to an historic European Cup victory and a then world record of nine league championships in a row, Billy knows he will never walk alone …